Under the Sea

Sperm Whales
and other
Deep-water
Life

Sally Morgan

QEB Publishing

Copyright © QEB Publishing 2008

First published in the United States in 2008 by
QEB Publishing Inc.
23062 La Cadena Drive
Laguna Hills, CA 92653

www.qeb-publishing.com

Library of Congress Number: 2008011386

ISBN 978 1 59566 568 3

Author Sally Morgan
Consultant Camilla de la Bedoyere
Editor Sarah Eason
Designed by Calcium
Picture Researcher Maria Joannou
Illustrator Geoff Ward

Publisher Steve Evans
Creative Director Zeta Davies

Printed and bound in China

Picture credits
Key: T = top, B = bottom, C = center, L = left, R = right,
FC = front cover, BC = back cover

Alamy Images Phillip Augustavo 16B
Corbis Denis Scott FC, Ralph White 18-19,
Richard Cummins 16-17
Dreamstime 3, 10B
FLPA Minden Pictures/Norbert Wu 12B
Getty Images Brian J Skerry/National Geographic 11T,
Darlyne A Murawski/National Geographic 14-15,
Norbert Wu/Minden Pictures 12-13, 15, Peter David/Taxi 14,
Science Faction 5L, Toru Yamanaka/AFP 8B
Naturepl Bruce Rasner/Rotman 8-9
Photolibrary Australian Only 7T, Earth Scenes/Animals
Animals 10-11, Jim Watt/Pacific Stock 20-21, Joyce & Frank
Burek/Animals Animals 17T, Oxford Scientific 5R, 6-7, 6L,
18L, 20
Science Photo Library Dr Ken Macdonald 19R
Shutterstock 22-23, 24

Words in **bold** can be found in the
glossary on page 22.

Contents

Deep ocean

People splash and swim on the surface of the ocean, but its waters spread thousands of miles below. In these dark depths are huge underwater mountains and giant valleys.

Scientists explore the deep ocean in special **submersibles** that take them down to the *seabed*.

Plenty of light

Surface zone: 0 to 650 feet

Twilight zone: 650 to 3280 feet

A little light

No light

Dark zone: 3280 to over 16,404 feet

Seabed

Valley

There are many different layers in the ocean.

Apart from the surface layer, ocean water is icy cold and dark. The animals that live here have found ways of surviving in this difficult **environment**.

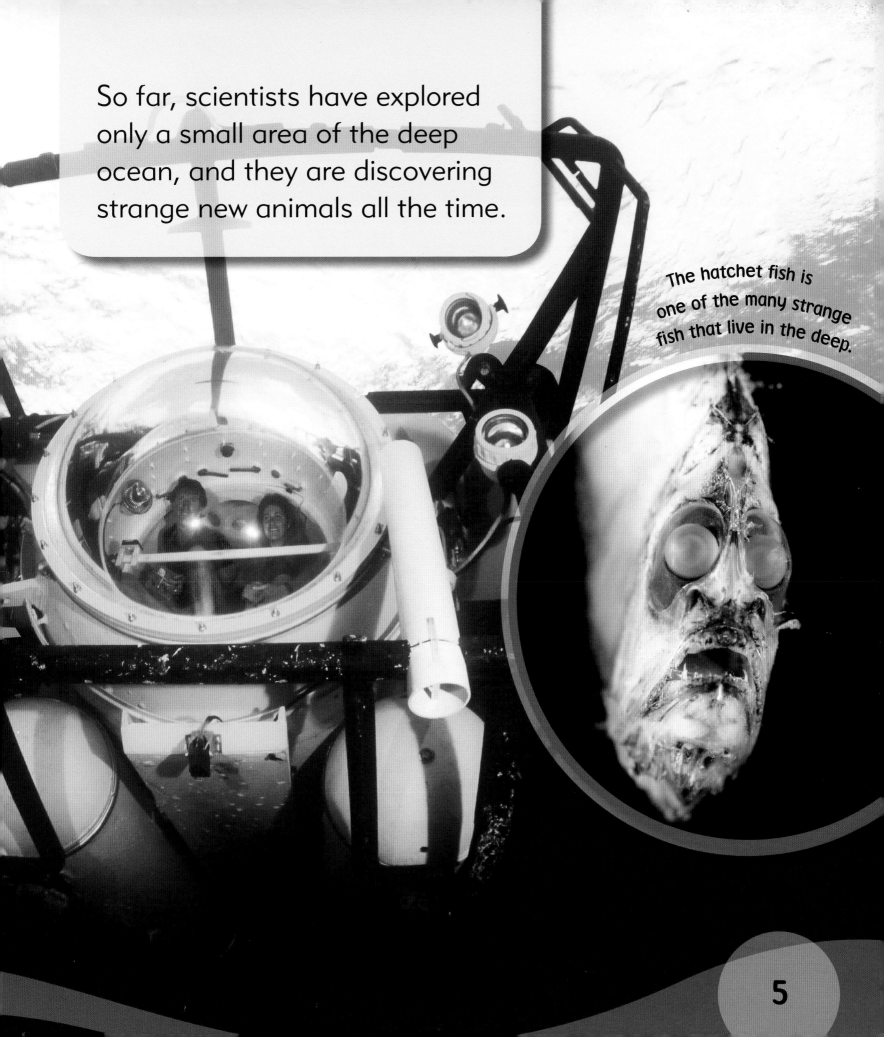

So far, scientists have explored only a small area of the deep ocean, and they are discovering strange new animals all the time.

The hatchet fish is one of the many strange fish that live in the deep.

Sperm whales

The sperm whale has a large, square head. It lives mostly near the surface of the ocean, but it can also dive into the deep zone.

The massive head of the sperm whale can be up to one-third of its length.

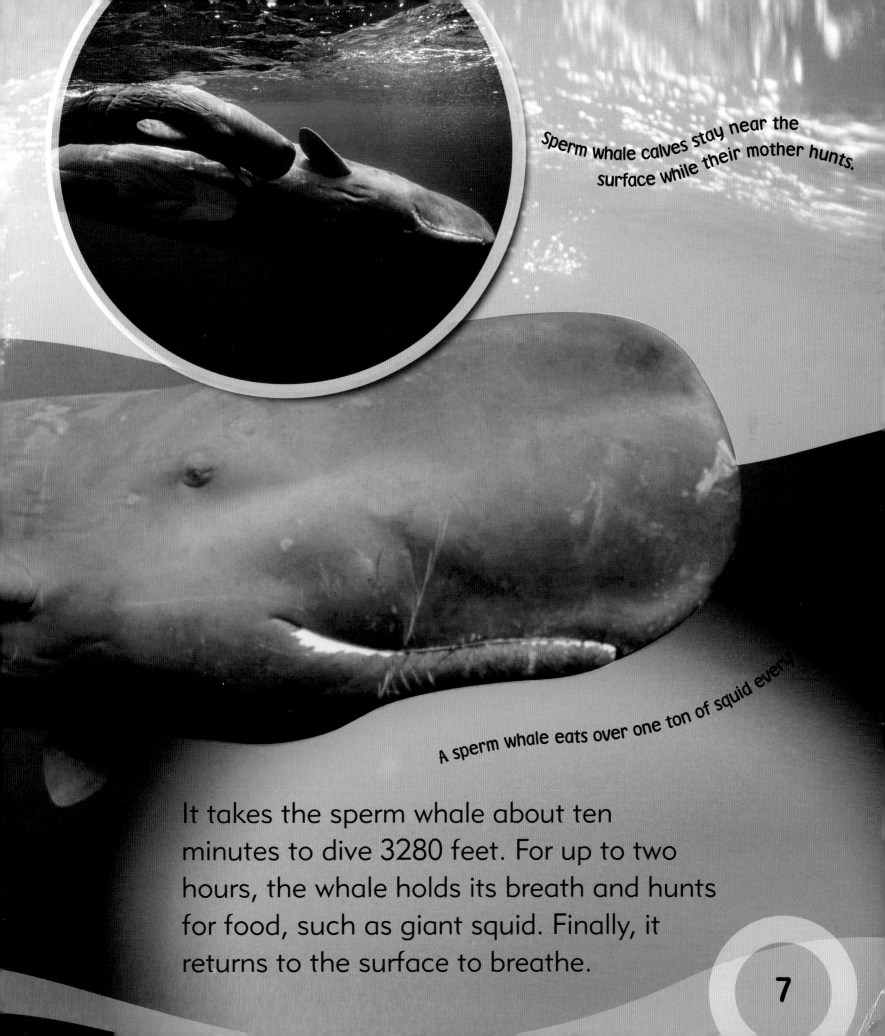

Sperm whale calves stay near the surface while their mother hunts.

A sperm whale eats over one ton of squid every

It takes the sperm whale about ten minutes to dive 3280 feet. For up to two hours, the whale holds its breath and hunts for food, such as giant squid. Finally, it returns to the surface to breathe.

Megamouth sharks

This shark was first discovered in 1976. Since then, only about 40 have been seen. It lives in deep water, where it is dark and very cold.

The megamouth shark is so called because of its huge mouth and rubbery lips. It swims slowly with its mouth wide open. This lets the shark take in massive amounts of water to trap **prey**, such as **shrimps**, in its **gills**.

The megamouth shark's mouth is so large, it could swallow small children.

Unlike other sharks, which have **muscular** bodies, the megamouth shark has a flabby body. It does not need to swim quickly to catch fish, which is why its muscles are weaker than most other sharks.

The megamouth shark has a large head. Its body grows to about 16 feet long—about as long as a car.

Giant squid

Giant squid grow to about 39 feet long and weigh as much as one ton—that's as long as a bus and as heavy as a station wagon!

Only a few people have seen a living giant squid, but their dead bodies are sometimes washed up on beaches.

The eye of the giant squid is as large as a dinner plate. This helps it to see its prey in gloomy water.

teeth

Squid have eight arms and two long **tentacles** covered in suckers. The suckers help the squid to hold on to slippery prey. Giant squid are fearsome hunters and will even attack a sperm whale.

Giant squid suckers are filled with sharp teeth.

Viperfish and gulper eels

It is hard to find food in the ocean's deepest zone. Viperfish and gulper eels lurk in the waters, waiting for prey to pass or a dead creature to sink from the surface waters.

The gulper eel has a hinged mouth, which can open wide to swallow prey larger than itself.

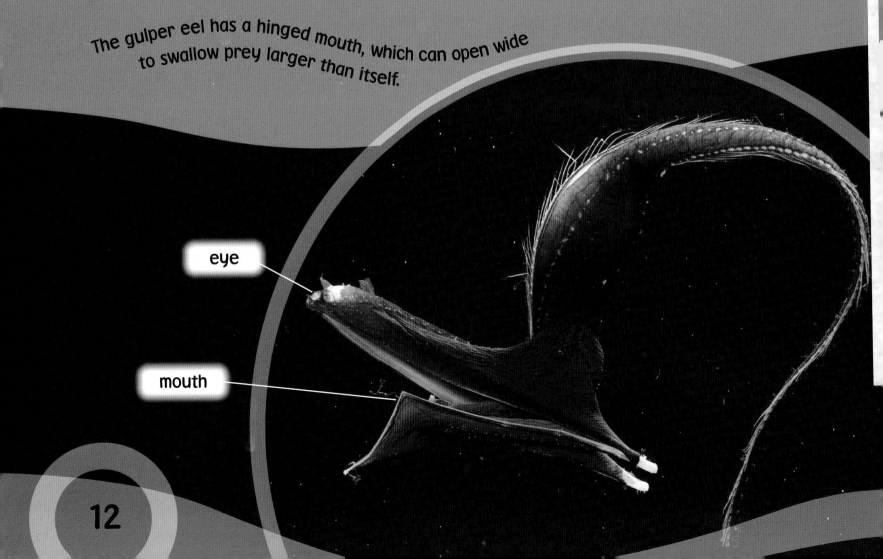

eye

mouth

Viperfish and gulper eels have knife-like teeth that grip prey so it cannot escape. Their huge stomach stretches so they can gobble up passing prey of any size.

The viperfish's mouth is full of long, razor-sharp teeth.

Angler fish

The angler fish lives in the darkest depths of the ocean. It has a long **spine**, which dangles from the top of its head. At the end of the spine is a light. The angler fish uses the light to attract its prey. The light is made by tiny creatures called **bacteria**, which live at the end of the spine.

In the darkness, other fish swim towards the angler fish's glowing light—and the fish snaps them up.

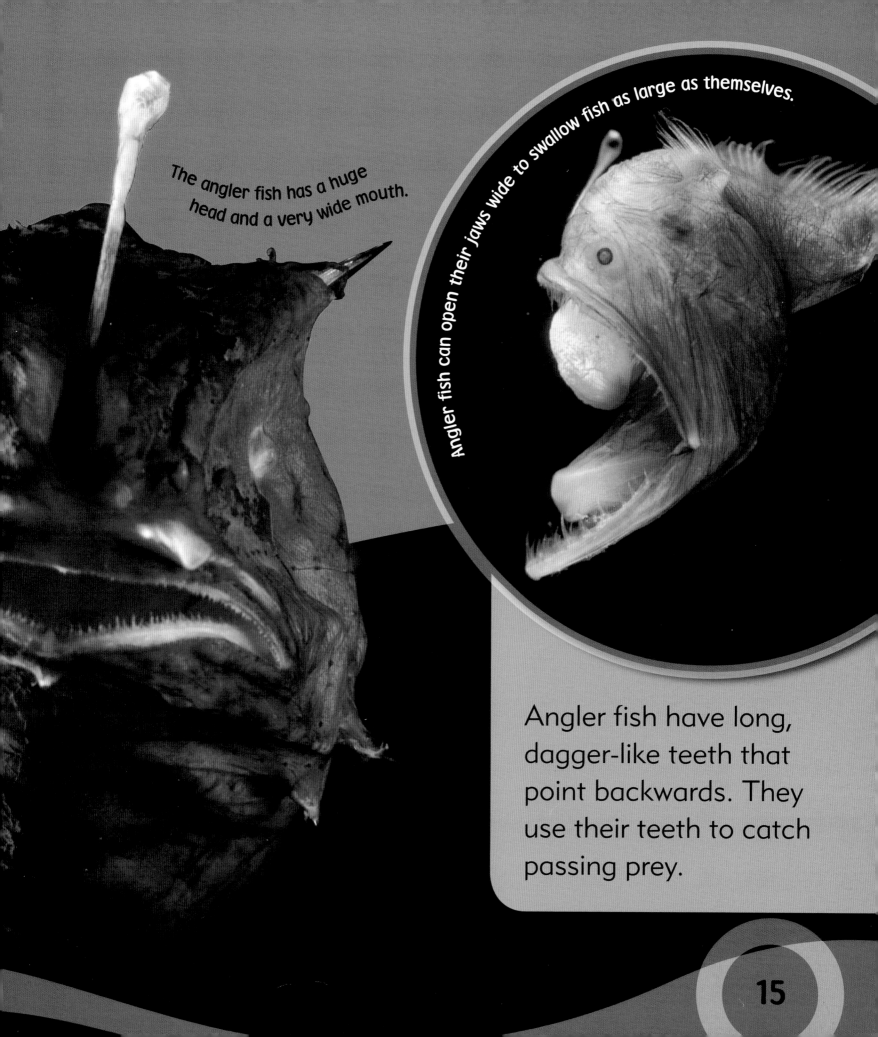

The angler fish has a huge head and a very wide mouth.

Angler fish can open their jaws wide to swallow fish as large as themselves.

Angler fish have long, dagger-like teeth that point backwards. They use their teeth to catch passing prey.

15

Spider crabs

Spider crabs have small bodies and ten very long legs. The Japanese spider crab's legs are up to 6.5 feet long, but its body is only the size of a dinner plate.

In the jet-black darkness, spider crabs use their legs as feelers to find their way around.

The body of the crab is covered by a tough shell.

Each leg ends in a small claw.

Spider crabs live on the seabed. They **scavenge**, feeding on dead animals that drop from the surface waters.

Giant tube worms

Strange creatures live on the deep-ocean seabed, around **hot water vents**. These are places where extremely hot water gushes from gaps in the rocks.

Hundreds of giant tube worms live around a hot water vent.

Giant tube worms are taller than an adult person.

Fish and crabs eat giant tube worms.

Giant tube worms grow to more than 6.5 feet long. They live inside a tough tube that they make themselves. Giant tube worms feed on bacteria that live inside them. The worms are then eaten by crabs and other deep-sea life.

19

Nautiluses

The nautilus has lived in the world's deep oceans for millions of years. It is a type of **mollusc** and is related to the squid. It is called a head-foot animal because its feet (the tentacles) are joined to its head.

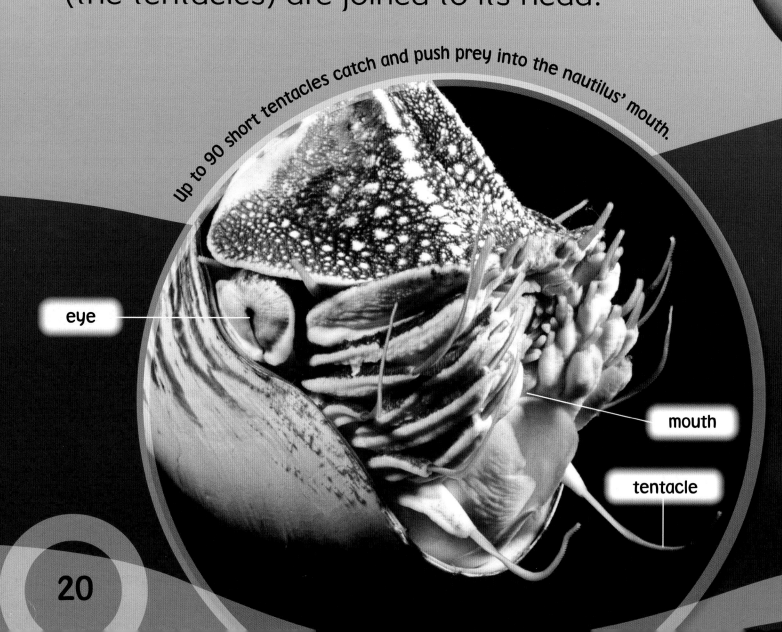

Up to 90 short tentacles catch and push prey into the nautilus' mouth.

eye

mouth

tentacle

Although the nautilus has a large eye, it does not have good eyesight. It uses smell and touch to find food in the dark.

Nautiluses have red-and-white spiral shells, which help to camouflage them.

21

Glossary

bacteria tiny creatures that can only be seen through a microscope

camouflage colors and patterns on an animal's body that help it hide in its environment

dark zone depths of the ocean where there is no light

environment the area in which an animal or plant lives

gill an opening in an underwater animal's body through which it breathes

hot water vents openings in the deep seabed where hot water gushes out

mollusc a sea creature, that has a soft body and often a hard shell

muscular to have strong muscles

prey an animal that is hunted by other animals

scavenge to search for dead animals to feed on

shrimp a small sea creature with a shell around its body

spine a long, sharp point

submersible vehicle used to explore underwater

surface zone upper layer of the ocean

tentacle a long, armlike limb of a sea creature. It is used for feeling and holding, and sometimes for stinging

twilight zone middle layer of the ocean

Index

Ideas for teachers and parents

- Animals of the deep cannot be kept in aquariums. To see photos and videos of these animals, visit a website such as Woods Hole Oceanographic Institution at www.whoi.edu* or Into the Abyss at www.pbs.org/wgbh/nova/abyss/mission/*. There is video of the sperm whale on www.arkive.org*. Many documentaries, such as *The Blue Planet: Seas of Life* from the BBC, have been made about creatures of the deep. The series can be watched on DVD.

- There are many food chains in the oceans. Using information from this book and from the Internet, ask children to draw a food chain using arrows to show the flow of energy—when one animal eats another.

- Encourage children to think up fun stories and poems about the sperm whale and its life in the deep ocean.

- Ask children to draw a picture showing the different animals that can be found around a hot water vent, such as giant tube worms and spider crabs.

- The ocean is under threat from global warming and water pollution, as well as over-fishing. Find out more about these threats from other books and the Internet.

- Make a word search using the different ocean-related vocabulary in this book.

* Web information is correct at time of going to press. However, the publishers cannot accept liability for any information or links found on third-party websites.